# Thai
## Noodles & Snacks

Nongkran Daks and Alexandra Greeley

D1806564

For light bites, exotic appetizers and simple one-dish meals, nothing beats the spicy, sweet and tantalizing flavors of Thai noodles and snacks. Prepare the perfect Pad Thai or Tender Beef Noodle Soup as well as snacks such as Spring Rolls, Golden Cups and Spicy Pork Satay. The clear instructions and step-by-step photographs in this book ensure delicious results every time.

PERIPLUS EDITIONS
Singapore • Hong Kong • Indonesia

# Basic Thai Ingredients

Dried finger-length chilies

Bird's-eye chilies

Fresh finger-length chilies

Dried bird's-eye chilies

**Chilies** come in many shapes and sizes. Fresh **finger-length chilies** are moderately hot. Tiny red, green or yellow-orange **bird's-eye chilies** are fiery hot. **Dried chilies** are usually cut into lengths and soaked in warm water to soften before use.

**Coconut milk** can be bought fresh from local wet markets and is also available canned and in packets. It comes in varying consistencies and you will need to adjust the thickness by adding water as needed. In general, you should add 1 cup of water to 1 cup of canned or packet coconut cream to obtain thick coconut milk, and 2 cups of water to 1 cup of coconut cream to obtain thin coconut milk.

**Coriander** is an indispensable herb and spice in Thai cooking. **Coriander seeds** are roasted and then ground in spice pastes. **Coriander roots** are used in the same way, while **coriander leaves** (also known as cilantro or Chinese parsley) are used as a herb and a garnish.

**Curry powder** is a commercial spice blend that generally includes ground cumin seeds, coriander seeds, turmeric root, ginger, cinnamon and cloves. Different combinations vary in color and flavor and are used for different types of curries—meat, fish or chicken. Use an all-purpose blend if a specific curry powder is not available. Store curry powder in an air-tight container in the refrigerator.

**Dried chinese sausages**, or *lap cheong*, are perfumed with rose-flavored wine. Generally sold in pairs, these sausages keep without refrigeration and are sliced and cooked with other ingredients rather than eaten on their own. They should not be eaten raw. Substitute any sweet, dried sausage or meat jerky.

**Dried prawns** are tiny, orange prawns that have been dried in the sun. They come in different sizes. Available in Asian markets, they should look orangy-pink and plump; avoid any with a grayish appearance or an unpleasant smell. Dried prawns will keep for several months.

**Dried shrimp paste,** which is called *kapee* in Thai and is known as *belachan* in Singapore and Malaysia, is a dense mixture of fermented ground shrimp that must be toasted before use—either wrapped in foil and dry-roasted in a pan or toasted over a gas flame. It is sold in dried blocks wrapped in paper or plastic in most Asian food stores.

**Fish sauce** is made from salted, fermented fish or shrimp. Good quality fish sauce is golden-brown in color and has a salty tang. It is available in bottles in most supermarkets.

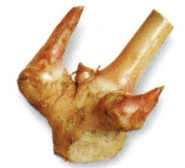

**Galangal** (*lengkuas*) is an aromatic root that is similar in appearance to ginger and a member of the same family. It adds a distinct flavor to Thai curries, and most stores now sell it fresh. It can be sliced and kept sealed in the freezer for several months.

**Garlic chives** or *gu cai*, also known as Chinese chives, have long, green flat leaves that resemble thin spring onions. They have a strong garlicky flavor and are added to noodle or stir-fried dishes during the final stages of cooking. If you cannot get them, use spring onions or regular chives.

**Kaffir limes** are small limes with a very rough and intensely fragrant skin, but virtually no juice. The skin or rind is often grated and used as a seasoning. Fragrant **kaffir lime leaves** are added whole to soups and curries or finely shredded and added to salads or deep-fried fish cakes, giving a wonderfully tangy taste to these dishes. They are available frozen or dried in Asian food stores; frozen leaves are much more flavorful than dried ones.

**Lemongrass** is a highly aromatic herb. The tough outer layers of the stem should be peeled away and only the pale, inner heart of the thick end are used.

**Oyster sauce** is a flavorful soy-based sauce made with oyster extract—a Cantonese specialty. A vegetarian version is available, and is sometimes sold as "mushroom oyster sauce" or "oyster-flavored sauce". If you do not like monosodium glutamate, choose your

Glass noodles
(*tang hoon*)

Fresh yellow wheat
noodles (*mee*)

Dried rice vermicelli
(*beehoon*)

Flat rice stick noodles
(*kway teow*)

**Noodles** are a universal favorite in Thailand. **Fresh yellow wheat noodles** are thick, spaghetti-like noodles made from wheat flour and egg. Substitute fresh spaghetti or fettucini if you cannot find them. **Dried rice vermicelli** (*mifen* or *beehoon*) are very fine rice threads that must be plunged into hot water to soften before use. **Rice stick noodles** (also known as "river noodles", *kway teow* or *hofun*) are wide, flat rice noodles sold fresh in Asian markets. If not available, use **dried rice stick noodles** instead. **Glass noodles**, also known as cellophane or bean thread noodles, are thin, clear strands made from mung bean starch and water. They are sold in dried form and must be soaked in warm water for 15 minutes to soften.

brand carefully as most are laden with this additive. Oyster sauce is available in most supermarkets. Soy sauce or Worcestershire sauce may be substituted although the flavor will not be the same.

**Plum sauce** is a sweet sauce made from plums, vinegar, sugar and a dash of chilies. It is sold in jars or cans in the supermarket.

**Palm sugar** is made from the distilled juice of various palm fruits and varies in color from golden to dark brown. It has a rich flavor similar to dark brown sugar or maple syrup, which make good substitutes.

**Preserved salted radish** or *chai poh* is pickled and dried Japanese radish or daikon. Added to dishes for its crunchy texture and salty flavor, it keeps almost indefinitely and is available from Asian markets.

**Star anise** is a dried brown seed pod with 8 woody petals, each with a shiny black seed inside, which has the flavor of cinnamon and aniseed. Use whole and remove from the dish before serving.

**Tamarind pulp** is the fruit of the tamarind tree seed

| Regular soy sauce | Dark soy sauce | Sweet black soy sauce |

**Soy sauce** is brewed from soybeans and wheat fermented with salt. It is a clear brown liquid with a salty taste and is used as a table condiment and cooking seasoning. **Dark soy sauce** is denser and less salty, with a malty tang. **Sweet black soy sauce** is a thick, fragrant sauce used in marinades and sauces. It is not widely available in the West but can be approximated by adding $1/_2$ teaspoon dark brown sugar to 1 tablespoon of normal dark soy sauce. Hoisin sauce also makes a good substitute.

**Wood ear mushrooms** have very little flavor and are added to dishes for their crunchy texture and as a meat substitute. They are sold dried in plastic packets in Asian supermarkets and comes in small, crinkly sheets. Soak them in water before using. Wash well and discard any hard bits that remain after soaking.

**Yellow bean paste** is similar to Japanese miso paste and is made from fermented yellow soybeans. It is an important seasoning in Asian dishes and is slightly sweet. "Sweet" and "hot" salted soy beans have added sugar and chili. Bean paste is sold in cans and jars.

pod. It is sold dried in packets or jars and generally still has some seeds and pod fibers mixed in with the dried pulp. It is used as a souring agent in many dishes. The dried pulp should be mixed with a small amount of warm water, mashed with the fingers, then strained to obtain **tamarind juice,** which is then added to sauces or spice mixes.

**Tapioca flour** is also known as cassava or manioc flour. This starch from the cassava root is used as a thickening agent like cornstarch. Combined with rice flour, it adds a translucent sheen and chewiness to cakes.

Available in Asian food markets. Cornstarch may be used as a substitute.

**Thai basil** (*horapa*) tastes rather like Italian sweet basil with a hint of anise and is used in red and green curries. It is available year round.

# Dips, Sauces and Condiments

Although rice is a mainstay at the Thai table, rice flour, egg or mung bean noodles are almost as widespread. Thai cooks have taken this Chinese import—the noodle—and created numerous delectable dishes, from stir-fries and salads to soups and delicate snacks. The following dips, pastes, sauces and side dishes are either recipes in their own right or basic components of other recipes featured later in this book.

## Sweet and Hot Plum Sauce (Nam Jim)

125 ml ($^1/_2$ cup) water
200 g (1 cup) sugar
125 ml ($^1/_2$ cup) vinegar
1 red finger-length chili, finely chopped
3 cloves garlic, peeled and finely chopped
2 tablespoons plum sauce or Japanese apricot sauce

1 Combine the water, sugar and vinegar in a small saucepan. Bring to a boil over high heat, then reduce the heat to low. Cook until the mixture begins to thicken, about 40 minutes.
2 Add the red chili, garlic and apricot sauce. Stir a few times. Remove from the heat and cool before serving.
3 Serve as a dip for Golden Sacks (Tung Thong) (page 26).

## Cucumber Salad (Ajaad)

2 tablespoons sugar
1 teaspoon salt
90 ml ($^1/_3$ cup) warm water
2 tablespoons vinegar
3 shallots, thinly sliced
1 red finger-length chili, sliced diagonally
1 small cucumber, peeled, quartered lengthwise and thinly sliced

1 Dissolve the sugar and salt in the water. Add the vinegar.
2 Place the shallots and the chili slices on top of the cucumber in a serving bowl. Pour the sugar water mixture over the top.
3 Serve as an accompaniment to Thai Pork Sata (page 16) or Fish Cakes (Tod Man Pla—page 27).

# Red Curry Paste (Nam Prik Kang Phet)

1 tablespoon coriander
  seeds
3 dried red chilies,
  soaked 30 minutes
1 stalk lemongrass, ten-
  der inner part of bottom
  third only, thinly sliced
3 thin slices galangal
3 shallots, peeled and
  coarsely chopped
7 cloves garlic, peeled
1 teaspoon kaffir lime
  rind
1 teaspoon dried shrimp
  paste (*belachan*)
90 ml ($^1/_3$ cup) water, or
  more as needed

1 Roast the coriander seeds in a dry frying-pan over medium heat until fragrant, about 2 minutes. Combine all the ingredients in a blender and process until smooth.

2 Store unused portions in a tightly closed container. Leftovers keep well in the refrigerator or freezer. This paste is used in the preparation of Peanut Sauce (Nam Saté—page 16) and Fish Cakes (Tod Man Pla—page 27), but it can also be used for any kind of Thai red curry.

# Miang Kham Sauce

1 small onion, thinly sliced
1 tablespoon thinly sliced
  lemongrass (tender inner
  part of bottom third only)
1 tablespoon shredded
  fresh ginger
1 tablespoon dried shrimp
  paste (*belachan*)
90 g ($^1/_2$ cup) shredded
  coconut
30 g ($^1/_4$ cup) dried
  prawns
1$^1/_2$ teaspoons salt
500 ml (2 cups) plus
  125–180 ml ($^1/_2$–$^3/_4$
  cups) water
200 g (1 cup) palm sugar
Crushed roasted peanuts,
  to garnish

1 Roast the onions, lemongrass, ginger and shrimp paste at 120°C (250°F) until golden, about 15 minutes. Roast the coconut at 180°C (350°F) until golden brown, stirring often, about 10 minutes.

2 Put the onions, lemongrass, ginger, dried shrimp paste, dried prawns, coconut and salt into a blender and add 125 ml ($^1/_2$ cup) water gradually and process, adding more water if necessary. Process for a few seconds; the consistency does not need to be smooth.

3 Transfer the mixture to a large saucepan and add 500 ml (2 cups) water and the palm sugar. Bring the mixture to a boil over medium heat, then reduce the heat to medium–low and cook for 1 hour and 15 minutes, stirring occasionally. Remove from the heat and cool. Serve with Miang Kham (Lettuce Leaf Cups— page 10).

# Fresh Spring Rolls (Po Piah Sot)

2 dried chinese sausages
  (*lap cheong*)
1 tablespoon oil
2 eggs, lightly beaten
8 spring roll wrappers
1 cucumber, peeled and
  cut into strips
250 g (8 oz) firm bean-
  curd, cut into strips
8 spring onions, trimmed
250 g (2 cups) cooked
  crabmeat, leave some
  to garnish
250 g (8 oz) bean sprouts,
  blanched for 2 minutes

**Sauce**
250 ml (1 cup) water
100 g ($^1/_2$ cup) palm sugar
2 tablespoons tamarind
  pulp soaked in 60 ml
  ($^1/_4$ cup) water, mashed
  and strained to obtain
  the juice
90 g ($^2/_3$ cup) finely
  ground roasted peanuts
2 tablespoons Crispy
  Fried Shallots (see note)
1 tablespoon fish sauce
1 tablespoon sweet black
  soy sauce

1 tablespoon oyster sauce
1 teaspoon salt
4 teaspoons cornstarch
  mixed with 60 ml
  ($^1/_4$ cup) water
$^1/_4$ teaspoon five spice
  powder
45 g ($^1/_4$ cup) dry-
  roasted sesame seeds
  (see note below)

Serves 8
Preparation time: **20 mins**
Assembling time: **20 mins**

**1** Steam the dried chinese sausages for 5 minutes, cool and cut into 8 strips lengthwise.
**2** Heat the oil in a wok or skillet over medium heat and fry the eggs into an omelet.
Cut the omelet into 8 long pieces and set aside.
**3** Place a spring roll wrapper on a flat surface and put a piece of sausage, omelet,
cucumber, beancurd, spring onion, 2 tablespoons of crabmeat and some bean sprouts
on the wrapper. Roll the wrapper up tightly. Repeat until you use all the wrappers.
**4** To make the Sauce, combine all the ingredients, except the sesame seeds, in a
saucepan. Cook over medium heat until the mixture boils; stir a few times. Add the
sesame seeds when the mixture begins to thicken. Transfer to a serving dish.
**5** Serve rolls as they are, or steam the rolls for 1 to 2 minutes in a steamer or
microwave oven. Garnish each roll with some crabmeat and serve the Sauce on the
side or drizzle on top.

**Crispy Fried Shallots** are readily available in packets or jars in most supermarkets and
Asian food stores. To make them at home, thinly slice several cloves of shallots as
desired and stir-fry in hot oil over low heat for 1–2 minutes, stirring constantly, until
golden brown and crispy. Remove with a slotted spoon and drain on paper towels.

Dry-roast the **sesame seeds** by heating a frying pan over medium heat, add the seeds,
and toss them continually for 2–3 minutes until they begin to brown, ensuring they're
removed from heat before they begin to pop and burn.

**Five spice powder** is a highly aromatic blend of Sichuan pepper, cinnamon bark, clove,
fennel and star anise, ground to a fine powder and used to season stir-fried foods,
in marinades and for sauces.

# Lettuce Leaf Cups
## (Miang Kham)

The trick to enjoying this traditional Thai snack is in sampling a bit of everything in the leaf cup—the combined flavors and textures make this a real treat. You may store any unused sauce in a tightly sealed container in the refrigerator or freezer.

1 lime or lemon, peeled and finely diced
5 cm (2 in) fresh ginger, peeled and diced
1 shallot, peeled and diced
30 g ($^1/_4$ cup) dried prawns
1 tablespoon thinly sliced red chilies
50 g ($^1/_3$ cup) roasted unsalted peanuts, skins removed, crushed
50 g ($^1/_2$ cup) dry-roasted grated coconut (see note below)
10 small pieces leafy green lettuce (about 150 g)
250 ml (1 cup) Miang Kham Sauce (page 5)

**1** Arrange the leaf cup ingredients in separate piles on a serving tray. Add the crushed peanuts to the Miang Kham Sauce and pour into a small dish.
**2** To serve, make a triangular cone from a leaf and fill the cone with 1 teaspoon coconut. Add 1 piece of each of the other ingredients. Spoon $^1/_2$ teaspoon of the Sauce over the contents and fold the leaf over to cover the filling before eating.

Heat a wok over very low heat, add the **grated coconut** and fry over very low heat, tossing them continually, until fragrant and golden brown, about 10 minutes. Set aside to cool before using.

Serves 12
Preparation and Cooking time: **2 hours**

# Steamed Prawn Dumplings
## (Khanom Jeeb)

30 circular wonton wrappers (see note)

3 tablespoons Garlic Oil (see note)

60 ml ($^1/_4$ cup) red rice vinegar with sliced red chilies

**Filling**

3 cloves garlic, peeled

3 fresh coriander roots

10 black peppercorns

200 g (1 cup) minced pork

180 g ($^3/_4$ cup) finely chopped fresh prawn meat

1 small onion, peeled and finely chopped

6 water chestnuts, peeled finely chopped

1 tablespoon cornstarch

1 tablespoon sugar

1 teaspoon fish sauce

1 teaspoon soy sauce

$^1/_2$ teaspoon salt

Makes 30 dumplings
Preparation time: **30 mins**
Cooking time: **5 mins**

**1** To make the Filling, grind the garlic, coriander roots and peppercorns until fine. Combine this paste with the remaining Filling ingredients in a mixing bowl until well blended.

**2** Working with 1 wonton wrapper at a time, place 1 heaped teaspoon of the Filling in the center of the wrapper and gather the sides of the wrapper around the Filling, forming natural pleats. As you work, press on the Filling to pack it tightly.

**3** Tap each dumpling lightly to flatten the bottom and make it stand upright. Place the dumplings in a steamer basket over boiling water, cover and steam over high heat for 5 minutes. Brush the tops with Garlic Oil. Remove from the heat to a serving platter. To eat, dip in the red rice vinegar with sliced red chilies.

To make the **Garlic Oil**, heat 3 to 4 tablespoons oil in a small frying-pan over medium heat. Add the 2 tablespoons chopped garlic and stir-fry until crispy and brown. Or combine the oil and garlic and cook for 2 to 3 minutes in a microwave at medium heat.

**Wonton wrappers** are made from wheat dough, and come in a variety of sizes and thicknesses. They are filled with meat or vegetables, then steamed, fried or used in soups. Fresh or frozen wonton wrappers are available in most supermarkets.

Place 1 heaped teaspoon of the Filling in the center of each wonton wrapper.

Gather the sides of the wrapper around the Filling, forming natural pleats.

# Thai Crab Cakes (Puu Jaa)

120 g (1 cup) crabmeat, picked clean
100 g (¹/₂ cup) minced pork
1 medium potato, cooked and mashed
1 sprig fresh coriander leaves, finely chopped
2 cloves garlic, peeled and minced
1 teaspoon fish sauce
1 egg, lightly beaten
¹/₂ teaspoon salt
¹/₂ teaspoon freshly ground black pepper
4 clean crab shells
500 ml (2 cups) oil for deep-frying

**1** Combine the crabmeat, pork, taro root or potato, coriander leaves, garlic, fish sauce, egg, salt and pepper. Fill the crab shells with this mixture.
**2** Steam the shells over high heat for 15 minutes.
**3** Heat the oil in a wok over high heat. Fry the shells, meat side down, until brown.

If crab shells are not available, form little crab cake patties and pan fry over medium heat, 3–4 minutes on each side.

Serves 4
Preparation time: **15 mins**
Cooking time: **25 mins**

# Prawns in a Blanket (Kung Hom Pha)

2 fresh coriander roots
1 clove garlic, peeled
$^1/_2$ teaspoon salt
6 white peppercorns
1 teaspoon soy sauce
12 fresh medium prawns,
  peeled and deveined
  with tails intact
6 spring roll wrappers,
  cut in half
500 ml (2 cups) oil for
  deep-frying
250 ml (1 cup) Sweet
  and Hot Plum Sauce
  (Nam Jim—page 6)

1 Using a pestle and mortar or spice grinder, grind the coriander roots, garlic, salt and peppercorns until fine. Add the soy sauce. Marinate the prawns in this mixture for a few minutes.

2 Wrap each prawn in half a spring roll wrapper, covering the body of the prawn and leaving the tail exposed. Repeat the procedure until you use up the remaining wrappers and prawns.

3 Heat the oil in a saucepan over medium heat. Deep-fry the prawns, a few at a time, until golden brown. Remove and drain on paper towels. Serve the prawns with the Sweet and Hot Plum Sauce.

Makes 12
Preparation time: **15 mins**
Cooking time: **10 mins**

# Thai Pork Satay (Saté Muu)

1 tablespoon sweet black soy sauce
500 g (1 lb) pork loin, cut into cubes
24 bamboo skewers
Coconut milk for basting

**Marinade**
1 onion, coarsely chopped
3 cloves garlic, peeled
1 stalk lemongrass, tender inner part of bottom third only, sliced
3 slices fresh ginger
1 teaspoon turmeric powder

2 teaspoon salt
1 tablespoon tamarind pulp soaked in 2 tablespoons water, mashed and strained to obtain the juice
1 tablespoon palm sugar
2 tablespoons oil
90 ml ($^1/_3$ cup) water, or more as needed

**Peanut Sauce (Nam Saté )**
2 tablespoons oil
2 tablespoons Red Curry Paste (page 5)
50 g ($^1/_2$ cup) Crispy Fried Shallots (see note)

375 ml (1$^1/_2$ cups) coconut milk
90 g ($^2/_3$ cup) roasted peanuts, coarsely ground
2 tablespoons palm sugar
$^1/_2$ tablespoon tamarind pulp soaked in 1 tablespoon water, mashed and strained to obtain the juice
1 teaspoon salt

Makes 60 sticks
Preparation time: 30 mins plus 2 hours soaking
Cooking time: 30 mins

1 Combine the Marinade ingredients in a blender and process until smooth. Pour the mixture into a large bowl.

2 Stir in the sweet black soy sauce and add the pork cubes. Marinate the meat for at least 2 hours.

3 To make the Peanut Sauce, heat the oil in a wok over high heat. Add the Red Curry Paste and Crispy Fried Shallots and stir until fragrant, about 3 minutes. Add the remaining ingredients and stir well. Reduce the heat to low and cook until the mixture begins to thicken; thin with some water if it gets too thick. Remove from the heat and place in a serving dish.

4 Thread 3 to 4 pieces of meat onto each skewer. Cook over a charcoal fire or under a grill (broiler) until brown. Baste each side once with coconut milk or oil while cooking. Serve with the Peanut Sauce and Cucumber Salad (Ajaad—page 5).

Crispy Fried Shallots are readily available in packets or jars in most supermarkets and Asian food stores. To make them at home, thinly slice several cloves of shallots as desired and stir-fry in hot oil over low heat for 1–2 minutes, stirring constantly, until golden brown and crispy. Remove with a slotted spoon and drain on paper towels.

# Crispy Rice Crackers with Dip
## (Khao Tang Na Tang)

500 ml (2 cups) oil
10–12 puffed rice cakes (purchased, see note)
1 dried red chili, soaked 20 minutes
1 fresh coriander stem and root, minced
4 cloves garlic, peeled
1 teaspoon black peppercorns
375 ml (1 1/2 cups) coconut milk
200 g (1 cup) minced pork
125 g (1/2 cup) peeled and coarsely chopped fresh prawn meat
90 g (2/3 cup) ground toasted peanuts
1 tablespoon tomato paste or ketchup
2 tablespoons palm sugar, shaved or crumbled
1 tablespoon fish sauce
1/2 teaspoon salt
2 tablespoons thinly sliced shallots
1 sprig fresh coriander leaves, coarsely chopped
1 red finger-length chili, deseeded and thinly sliced

1 Heat the oil in a wok or large saucepan over medium heat. Fry the rice cakes, a few at a time, until lightly golden, turning to brown both sides. Remove and set aside on paper towels to drain.

2 Using a mortar and pestle, or spice grinder, grind the chili, coriander root, garlic and peppercorns until fine.

3 Heat the coconut milk in a saucepan over medium heat until it begins to boil. Add the spice mixture and stir a few times. Add the pork and prawn meat and stir until well mixed. Add the peanuts and continue cooking for 5 minutes. Add the tomato paste, palm sugar, fish sauce and salt and continue to cook for 15 minutes more. The consistency should resemble chili con carne.

4 Remove the mixture from the heat and put into a serving bowl. Sprinkle with the shallots, coriander leaves and chili. Place the bowl on a platter and surround with the rice cakes. To serve, spoon the dip over each piece of cake.

**Puffed rice cakes**, made from puffed rice, is sold as a healthy snack food in North America and other Western countries. In North America, they are manufactured in several different flavors, and are becoming increasingly popular as a portable low-calorie snack. Puff rice is usually made by heating rice kernels under high pressure in the presence of steam.

Serves 6 to 8
Preparation time: 20 mins
Cooking time: 30 mins

# Chicken Curry Puffs (Kari Puff)

250 g (8 oz) packet
    frozen puff pastry
750 ml (3 cups) oil

**Stuffing**
500 g (1 lb) boneless,
    skinless chicken breast,
    diced or minced
1 teaspoon salt
1 tablespoon soy sauce
5 fresh coriander roots
$1/2$ teaspoon white
    peppercorns
5 cloves garlic, peeled
2 tablespoons oil
2 teaspoons curry powder
3 tablespoons Worch-
    estershire sauce
1 teaspoon salt
1 medium onion, diced
250 g (8 oz) boiled pota-
    toes, diced

Makes 24
Preparation time: **45 mins**
Cooking time: **15 mins**

**1** Defrost the puff pastry sheets at room temperature for 20 to 30 minutes, according to instructions on label.
**2** To make the Stuffing, combine the chicken with the salt and soy sauce and set aside.
**3** Using a mortar and pestle, or spice grinder, grind the coriander roots, peppercorns and garlic until smooth. Heat the oil over medium heat until hot. Add the spice paste and stir-fry for 2 to 3 minutes, or until fragrant. Add the meat and continue to fry until the meat changes color. Add the curry powder, Worchestershire sauce and salt and stir well to combine.
**4** Add the onion and potatoes and continue cooking until the mixture looks dry. Set aside to cool.
**5** Roll out the pastry and cut into circles 10 cm (4 in) in diameter. Place 1 tablespoon of the Stuffing slightly off the center of each circle, fold each in half and pinch the edges to close.
**5** Heat the oil in a large skillet and deep-fry the puffs until golden, or bake at 200°C (400°F) for 12 minutes.

**Puff pastry** is a very light pastry made in layers that will expand when cooked, leaving large air pockets inside and is used for sweet or savory dishes. Available ready-made either chilled or frozen in supermarkets. Look for all-butter varieties for the best flavor.
The puffs can be made with many kinds of stuffing, including potatoes and taro root; you may also substitute diced or minced beef for the chicken. Or if you want a vegetarian version of this dish, replace the meat with beancurd.

Place 1 tablespoon of the Stuffing on the pastry, slightly off-center.

After folding the circle in half, lightly pinch the edges to seal the puff.

# Golden Cups (Kratong Thong)

Oil for deep-frying
Tartlet molds

**Batter**
225 g (1 1/2 cups) plain
  flour
1 egg
1/2 teaspoon salt
250 ml (1 cup) water

**Filling**
10 peppercorns
2 fresh coriander roots
3 cloves garlic, peeled
2 tablespoons oil
1 skinless chicken breast,
  diced to yield 60 g
  (1/2 cup) diced chicken
1 small onion, diced
300 g (2 cups) fresh or
  frozen corn kernels
2 tablespoons fish sauce
1 tablespoon sugar
Sprigs of fresh coriander
  leaves, to garnish
1 red finger-length chili,
  deseeded and cut into
  thin strips, to garnish

Makes 40 to 50
Preparation time: 30 mins
Assembling time: 30 mins

1 Mix all the Batter ingredients in a bowl until a smooth batter is obtained.

2 Heat the oil in a wok or saucepan over medium heat until hot. Using tongs, briefly dip a tartlet mold in the hot oil, then dip the bottom of the mold into the Batter to coat it well on the bottom side only. Return the coated mold to the oil and deep-fry until the cup detaches from the mold and turns golden brown, 1 to 2 minutes. Remove the cup from the oil and drain on paper towels. If the cup does not detach from the mold during deep-frying, remove the mold and cup together and set aside to cool on paper towels. The cup should come loose after about 5 minutes. Repeat to make cups with the remaining Batter.

3 To make the Filling, grind the peppercorns in a mortar or blender until fine. Combine with the coriader roots and garlic, and grind to a paste. Heat the oil in a wok or skillet over medium heat and stir-fry the ground mixture until fragrant, 1 to 2 minutes. Add the chicken and stir-fry until it changes color, then add the onion and corn kernels. Stir-fry the mixture for 3 to 4 minutes, seasoning with the fish sauce and sugar, until the mixture is cooked and well combined. Remove from the heat.

4 Spoon the Filling into the cups just before serving. Garnish each cup with the chopped coriander leaves and red chili slices.

For an interesting variation called "golden nests", use shredded potatoes or cooked and drained rice vermicelli—press a small portion into the wire mold and press the shreds or noodles into place with a second mold before frying.

Dip the outside of the mold into the Batter mixture.

Remove from the oil when light brown and leave to cool for 5 minutes.

# Steamed Mussels with Lemongrass

500 g (1 lb) mussels, cleaned
125 ml ($^1/_2$ cup) water
2 shallots, diced
1 stalk lemongrass, tender inner part of bottom third only, crushed and cut into lengths
$^1/_2$ teaspoon salt
$^1/_4$ teaspoon freshly ground black pepper
20 g ($^1/_2$ cup) Thai basil leaves

**Dipping Sauce**
2 cloves garlic, peeled
2 fresh coriander roots
2 or 3 red finger-length chilies
125 ml ($^1/_2$ cup) water
125 ml ($^1/_2$ cup) freshly squeezed lime juice
60 ml ($^1/_4$ cup) fish sauce
1 teaspoon salt
1 tablespoon sugar
2 tablespoons fresh coriander leaves, chopped

Serves 4 to 6
Preparation time: **15 mins**
Assembling time: **5 mins**

**1** To prepare the Dipping Sauce, use a pestle and mortar to pound the garlic, coriander roots and chilies until smooth. Combine this paste with the remaining Dipping Sauce ingredients in a mixing bowl and stir well.
**2** Discard any open mussels. Place the remainder in a wok and add the remaining ingredients. Cover and bring to a boil over high heat, cooking for 5 minutes. Remove from the heat and serve with the Dipping Sauce. To eat, remove the mussels from the shells and dip in the Sauce.

# Fried Corn Patties (Tod Man Khao Pote)

2 fresh coriander stems
  and roots
2 cloves garlic, peeled
$1/2$ teaspoon peppercorns
250 g (8 oz) minced pork
300 g (2 cups) fresh or
  frozen corn kernels or
  1 can (300 g/10 oz)
  canned corn kernels,
  drained

1 large egg
1 tablespoon plain flour
1 tablespoon tapioca
  flour or cornstarch
$1/2$ tablespoon soy sauce
$1/2$ tablespoon fish sauce
$1/2$ teaspoon salt
5 kaffir lime leaves, thinly
  sliced crosswise
500 ml (2 cups) oil

Serves 4 to 6
Preparation time: **15 mins**
Cooking time: **15 mins**

1 Using a pestle and mortar, pound the coriander stems and roots, garlic and peppercorns until fine. Transfer to a mixing bowl. Add the remaining ingredients, except the oil, and stir well.
2 Heat the oil in a wok or large skillet over medium–high heat. Shape 1 heaping tablespoon mixture into a patty. Carefully slide each patty into the oil and cook on both sides until brown. Remove from the oil with a slotted spoon. Drain on paper towels. Repeat until the batter is used up. Serve hot.

# Golden Sacks (Tung Thong)

3 fresh coriander roots
5 cloves garlic, peeled
  and finely chopped
5 black peppercorns
250 g (1 cup) finely
  chopped fresh prawns
200 g (1 cup) minced pork
120 g (4 oz) glass noodles,
  soaked 20 minutes,
drained and cut into
  lengths
6 water chestnuts, peeled
  and finely chopped
750 ml (3 cups) plus
  2 tablespoons oil
1 teaspoon salt
1/2 tablespoon fish sauce
30 small spring roll
wrappers
30 whole stalks spring
  onion, blanched
Sweet and Hot Plum
  Sauce (*Nam Jim*—page 6)

Serves 4 to 6
Preparation time: 20 mins
Cooking time: **15 mins**

1 Grind the coriander roots, garlic and peppercorns until fine. Transfer half of the paste to a mixing bowl. Add the prawns, pork, glass noodles, water chestnuts, salt, and fish sauce and stir well to combine.

2 Heat 2 tablespoons of oil in a wok or skillet over medium–high heat. Add the remaining paste and stir-fry until golden. Add the prawn and pork mixture and stir-fry for 4 or 5 minutes. Remove from the heat.

3 Place a spring roll wrapper on a flat surface and spoon 1 tablespoon of the mixture onto the center of the wrapper. Gather the edges together to form a small sack. Tie the sack with a stalk of spring onion and set aside. Repeat with the remaining wrappers.

4 Heat the 750 ml (3 cups) of oil in a wok over medium heat and gently put the sacks in the oil, a few at a time. Fry the sacks until golden brown. Remove with a slotted spoon. Drain on a wire rack. Serve with Sweet and Hot Plum Sauce (page 6).

# Thai Fish Cakes (Tod Man Pla)

500 g (1 lb) white fish fillets
60 ml ($^1/_4$ cup) Red Curry Paste (page 7)
1 tablespoon fish sauce
$^1/_2$ teaspoon salt
1 teaspoon sugar
6 kaffir lime leaves, very thinly sliced
2 tablespoons tapioca flour or cornstarch
2 tablespoons plain flour
1 egg
100 g ($^1/_2$ cup) very thinly sliced winged beans, long beans or green beans
750 ml (3 cups) oil for deep-frying

1 Process the fish in a food processor briefly until coarsely chopped, or slice and chop finely with a large knife. Combine the fish with the Red Curry Paste, fish sauce, salt, sugar, kaffir lime leaves, tapioca flour or cornstarch and plain flour in a large mixing bowl. Stir well until the mixture becomes sticky. Add the egg, stir several times, then add the beans. Mix well.

2 Heat the oil in a wok or frying pan over medium–high heat. Dip your hand in water to prevent sticking, then shape 1 heaped tablespoon mixture into a patty around 5 cm (2 in) round and 1 cm ($^1/_2$ in) thick. Carefully put each cake into the hot oil and fry until golden brown. Remove from the oil with a slotted spoon. Drain on paper towels. Serve with Cucumber Relish (Ajaad) (page 6).

Serves 4 to 6
Preparation time: **20 mins**
Cooking time: **15 mins**

# Tapioca Dumplings with Pork Filling

300 g (2 cups) dried tapioca pearls or tapioca flour
250 ml (1 cup) warm water

**Filling**

30 g ($^1/_4$ cup) diced preserved salted radish (page 4)
3 fresh coriander roots
4 cloves garlic, peeled
$^1/_2$ teaspoon black peppercorns
2 tablespoons oil
200 g (1 cup) minced pork
10 shallots, diced
100 g ($^1/_2$ cup) palm sugar
60 ml ($^1/_4$ cup) fish sauce
90 g ($^2/_3$ cup) ground roasted peanuts
4 tablespoons Garlic Oil (see note)
$2^1/_2$ liters (10 cups) water

**Garnish**

2 tablespoons fried garlic, as garnish
1 head leafy lettuce, leaves separated and rinsed
9 sprigs fresh coriander leaves

Makes 60
Preparation time: **50 mins**
Cooking time: **20 mins**

1 Combine the tapioca pearls or flour and warm water in a mixing bowl and stir with a wooden spoon until mixed. Knead into a soft dough. Cover with a moist cloth and set aside.

2 Wash the salted radish, squeeze dry and set aside. Using a pestle and mortar, pound the coriander roots, garlic and peppercorns until fine.

3 Heat the 2 tablespoons of oil over medium heat in a wok. Fry the pounded mixture until fragrant, about 3 minutes. Add the pork and keep stirring, breaking up any lumps. Add the onion and salted radish. Stir in the palm sugar and fish sauce and continue to cook until the liquid is almost evaporated. Add the peanuts. Stir until the Filling mixture thickens. Remove from the heat and cool.

4 To make the balls, dip your hands in cold water. Take about 1 teaspoon tapioca dough and shape it into a small ball, then flatten it. Place 1 teaspoon of the Filling in the center and gather the edges up to form a ball. Repeat to use up the remaining dough and Filling.

5 Use the Garlic Oil to oil a serving platter. Bring the $2^1/_2$ liters (10 cups) water to a boil in a large saucepan. Drop the tapioca balls into the water, about 10 pieces at a time. When they float to the surface, use a slotted spoon to scoop them out, place them on the serving platter and sprinkle with the fried garlic. Alternatively, steam the balls over high heat for 5 minutes. Serve with the lettuce leaves and fresh coriander leaves.

To make the **Garlic Oil**, heat 3 to 4 tablespoons oil in a small frying-pan over medium heat. Add the 2 table-spoons chopped garlic and stir-fry until crispy and brown. Or combine the oil and garlic and cook for 2 to 3 min-utes in a microwave at medium heat.

# Fried Spring Rolls (Po Piah Todd)

## Filling
500 g (1 lb) minced pork or chicken

100 g (4 oz) glass noodles, soaked 30 minutes, drained and cut into lengths (page 50)

2 tablespoons wood ear mushrooms

200 g (2 cups) shredded cabbage

250 g (8 oz) bean sprouts, blanched 2 minutes and coarsely chopped

1 carrot, grated

2 cloves garlic, peeled and finely chopped

2 tablespoons fresh coriander leaves, chopped

2 tablespoons fish sauce

1 tablespoon soy sauce

1 teaspoon salt

1 teaspoon ground white pepper

24 spring roll wrappers

1 tablespoon cornstarch mixed with enough water to form a paste

750 ml (3 cups) oil

## Sweet and Hot Sauce
60 ml ($^1/_4$ cup) water

100 g ($^1/_2$ cup) sugar

1 teaspoon salt

60 ml ($^1/_4$ cup) vinegar

$^1/_2$ teaspoon minced red chili

50 g ($^1/_3$ cup) roasted ground peanuts

1 To make the Sweet and Hot Sauce, bring the water, sugar and salt to a boil in a small saucepan. Reduce the heat to low and simmer for about 15 minutes. Remove from the heat. Stir in the vinegar and minced chili. Let cool and add the peanuts before serving.

2 Combine all the ingredients except the wrappers, cornstarch paste and oil in a mixing bowl. Lay a spring roll wrapper on a flat surface and place 2 tablespoons of the filling on the lower half of the wrapper. Fold the bottom edge up over the filling, then fold the right and left edges over the first fold, then roll tightly. Seal the edge of each roll with the cornstarch paste. Repeat until the wrappers and filling are finished.

3 Heat the oil in a wok over high heat. Place the rolls, a few at a time, into the oil and deep-fry until golden brown. Remove with a slotted spoon or tongs. Drain on paper towels. Serve hot with the Sweet and Hot Sauce.

Spring roll wrappers are thin sheets of light, pliable pastry made from wheat flour, eggs and salt. These wrappers are usually used to wrap a variety of fillings, then deep-fried until golden brown. They are available both fresh and frozen in well-stocked supermarkets and Asian markets. They are also sold in the West as egg roll wrappers, and are often called skins, rather than wrappers in Asia. Indonesia or Filipino lumpia skins are good substitutes.

Makes 24 rolls
Preparation time: 30 mins plus 30 mins soaking
Cooking time: 20 mins

# Fried Beancurd with Sweet and Hot Sauce (Taohu Saweai)

500 g (1 lb) firm bean-
curd, cut into 8 pieces
150 g (1 cup) plain flour
1 teaspoon salt
1 teaspoon freshly
ground black pepper
2 large eggs, lightly
beaten
120 g (2 cups) bread-
crumbs
500 ml (2 cups) oil

**Sweet and Hot Sauce**
60 ml (¹/₄ cup) water
100 g (¹/₂ cup) sugar
60 ml (¹/₄ cup) apple
cider vinegar
1 teaspoon salt
1 teaspoon *sambal oelek*
(Indonesian chili paste)
2 tablespoons plum
sauce or Japanese
apricot sauce

Serves 4
Preparation time: 40 mins
Cooking time: 15 mins

1 Wrap the beancurd pieces in several layers of paper towels, applying light pressure to remove excess water. Set aside on dry paper towels.

2 To make the Sweet and Hot Sauce, combine all the ingredients except the chili paste and apricot sauce in a small pan. Cook over medium–low heat until the sauce becomes syrupy, about 30 minutes. Stir in the *sambal oelek* (chili paste) and apricot sauce. Remove from the heat and set aside.

3 To prepare the beancurd, mix the flour, salt and pepper in a small bowl. Dredge the beancurd pieces in the flour mixture, then dip into the egg mixture and coat with the breadcrumbs.

4 Heat the oil in a wok over medium–high heat. Deep-fry several pieces of beancurd at a time until golden brown. Remove from the oil with a slotted spoon. Drain on paper towels. Serve with the Sweet and Hot Sauce.

**Sambal oelek** is a hot chili paste made from chilies, salt and vinegar, usually with the chili seeds left in. A spoonful of sambal oelek will add heat to any dish. Available from supermarkets. Any other type of spicy chili sauce may also be used

# Chicken Noodle Soup
## (Kuay Tiaw Gai)

2 tablespoons fish sauce
500 g (1 lb) fresh rice stick noodles (*kway teow* or *hofun*)
  or 250 g (8 oz) dried rice stick noodles, blanched for
  2 minutes in boiling water and drained
250 g (8 oz) fresh bean sprouts, cleaned and rinsed,
  heads removed and blanched for 2 minutes
1 onion, thinly sliced crosswise
2 sprigs fresh coriander leaves, coarsely chopped
20 g (1 cup) Thai basil leaves (optional)
1 lime, cut into wedges

**Stock**
One whole chicken, about $1^1/_2$ kgs (2–3 lbs)
$1^1/_2$ liters (6 cups) chicken stock or water
1 small cinnamon stick
2 spring onions, cut in half
$2^1/_2$ cm (1 in) fresh ginger, grated
1 teaspoon salt
1 teaspoon sugar

**1** To make the Stock, combine all the ingredients in a
large stockpot. Bring the mixture to a boil over
medium heat, reduce the heat to low and cook for
about 1 hour. When ready to serve, lift the chicken
from the pot and leave to cool, then shred the meat.
Stir the fish sauce into the Stock.
**2** To serve, place some noodles in each soup bowl.
Garnish with the shredded chicken, bean sprouts,
onion slices, fresh coriander leaves and basil. Add
about 250 ml (1 cup) stock to each bowl. Serve each
bowl with a wedge of lime to squeeze over the top.

Serves 4 to 6
Preparation time: **20 mins**
Cooking time: **1 hour**

# Duck Noodle Soup (Kuay Tiaw Ped)

500 g (1 lb) fresh rice
stick noodles (*kway teow*
or *hofun*) or 250 g (8 oz)
dried rice stick noodles,
blanched for 2 minutes
in boiling water and
drained
2 tablespoons Garlic Oil
(see note)
500 g (1 lb) bean sprouts,
cleaned and rinsed,
heads removed and
blanched for 1 minutes
Half head leaf lettuce,
leaves separated and
rinsed
3 spring onions, thinly
sliced
Freshly ground white
pepper to taste
2 sprigs fresh coriander
leaves, chopped
60 ml ($^1/_4$ cup) chili-
vinegar, to garnish (see
note)
Crushed red finger-length
chilies, to garnish
(optional)

Serves 6 to 8
Preparation time: 20 mins
Cooking time: 1 hour
 40 mins

**Stock**
2 whole star anise
1 small cinnamon stick
1 whole duck (2 kgs/4
 lbs), cleaned
2$^1/_2$ liters (10 cups)
 water
5 fresh coriander roots,
 crushed
2$^1/_2$ cm (1 in) galangal

10 cloves garlic, peeled
 and crushed
1 teaspoon black pepper-
 corns
2 tablespoons rock sugar
60 ml ($^1/_4$ cup) mush-
 room soy sauce or dark
 soy sauce
60 ml ($^1/_4$ cup) fish sauce
1 tablespoon salt

1 To prepare the Stock, roast the star anise and the
cinnamon stick in a dry skillet over medium heat until
fragrant, 1 to 2 minutes. Combine the remaining Stock
ingredients in a large stockpot and bring to a boil over
medium heat. Reduce the heat to medium–low, cover
and cook the duck until tender, but not falling apart,
about 1$^1/_2$ hours. Remove the duck and allow to cool.
Strain the stock, discard the solids and return the
stock to the pot. Skim any fat from the surface. Keep
warm over low heat. Debone the duck and slice the
meat into bite-sized pieces. Set aside.
2 To serve, heat the noodles in boiling water to cover
until soft, about 1 minute, or heat in the microwave
for 2 minutes. Drain and place a portion of noodles
into individual soup bowls. Add 6 to 7 pieces of duck,
1 teaspoon Garlic Oil, bean sprouts and several lettuce
leaves. Garnish with spring onion, pepper and fresh
coriander leaves. Add 250 ml (1 cup) of the Stock and
serve with the Chili-Vinegar or crushed red chilies.

To make the **Chili-Vinegar**, slice several green chilies
into circles, put them in a small bowl and cover with
cider vinegar.

To make the **Garlic Oil**, heat 3 to 4 tablespoons oil in
a small frying-pan over medium heat. Add the 2 tablespoons chopped garlic and stir-fry until crispy and
brown. Or combine the oil and garlic and cook for
2 to 3 minutes in a microwave at medium heat.

# Tender Fragrant Beef Noodle Soup
## (Kuay Tiaw Nua Puai)

1$^1/_4$ liters (5 cups) water
500 g (1 lb) fresh rice stick noodles (*kway teow* or *hofun*) or 250 g (8 oz) dried rice stick noodles, blanched for 2 minutes in boiling water and drained
250 g (8 oz) fresh bean sprouts, blanched for 2 minutes
1$^1/_2$ tablespoons Garlic Oil (see note)
2 sprigs fresh coriander leaves, coarsely chopped
2 spring onions, finely sliced

2 tablespoons Chili-Vinegar (see note)

**Stock**
500 g (1 lb) oxtail or short ribs
500 g (1 lb) stewing beef
3 liters (12 cups) water
1 onion, cleaned but left unpeeled
1 tablespoon dark soy sauce
1$^1/_2$ tablespoons fish sauce
2 teaspoons salt
2 tablespoons soy sauce
10 cloves garlic, whole

1 small cinnamon stick
1 star anise
3 fresh coriander roots, crushed
$^1/_2$ celery root
$^1/_2$ teaspoon freshly ground black pepper
1 teaspoon sugar
2$^1/_2$ cm (1 in) galangal, crushed

Serves 4
Preparation time: **15 mins**
Cooking time: **2 hours**

**1** Combine the Stock ingredients in a large stockpot and bring to a boil over medium heat. Reduce the heat to low, cover and cook until the meat is very tender, about 1$^1/_2$ hours. Add more water if necessary.

**2** Meanwhile, in a large saucepan, heat 1$^1/_4$ liters (5 cups) water over medium heat. When the water boils, add the noodles, stir and cook for 1 minute or until tender. Drain in a colander.

**3** To serve, put a portion of the noodles and bean sprouts into individual soup bowls. Add 250 ml (1 cup) of the Stock and some meat to each bowl. Add 1 teaspoon Garlic Oil, a sprinkle of coriander leaves and spring onions. Serve with Chili-Vinegar, as desired.

To make the **Chili-Vinegar**, slice several green chilies into circles, put them in a small bowl and cover with cider vinegar.

To make the **Garlic Oil**, heat 3 to 4 tablespoons oil in a small frying-pan over medium heat. Add the 2 tablespoons chopped garlic and stir-fry until crispy and brown. Or combine the oil and garlic and cook for 2 to 3 minutes in a microwave at medium heat.

# Prawn and Pineapple Noodle Salad

250 g (8 oz) fresh or
  dried wheat noodles or
  fettucini
125 ml ($^1/_2$ cup) coconut
  milk
250 g (8 oz) fresh
  prawns, peeled and
  deveined
300 g (1 cup) crushed
  pineapple (fresh pine-
  apple is desirable)
1 spring onion, thinly
  sliced

**Dressing**

60 ml ($^1/_4$ cup) freshly
  squeezed lime juice
60 ml ($^1/_4$ cup) fish sauce
2 tablespoons sugar
3 cloves garlic, minced
2 tablespoons fresh ginger,
  grated

1 To make the Dressing, combine the lime juice, fish sauce, sugar, garlic and ginger in a mixing bowl and stir well. Set aside.

2 Bring 6 cups ($1^1/_2$ liters) of water to a boil in a pan. Add the dried noodles, bring to a boil again and cook for 3 to 4 minutes until the noodles are tender. If using fresh noodles, blanch briefly to revive them. Then drain, rinse in cold water and set aside to drain in a colander.

3 Heat the coconut milk in a saucepan over medium heat and when it begins to simmer, add the prawns and cook until just pink, about 3 minutes.

4 Arrange the noodles on a serving platter. Top with the prawns and pineapple and drizzle with the Dressing. Garnish with the spring onion before serving.

Serves 4
Preparation time: **15 mins**
Cooking time: **10 mins**

# Fried Rice Noodles with Prawns and Thai Basil

4 tablespoons oil
250 g (8 oz) fresh prawns, peeled and deveined
3 cloves garlic, minced
500 g (1 lb) fresh rice stick noodles (*kway teow* or *hofun*)
  or 250 g (8 oz) dried rice stick noodles, blanched for
  2 minutes in boiling water and drained
1 tablespoon sweet black soy sauce
2 tablespoons fish sauce
1 tablespoon oyster sauce
20 Thai basil leaves
2 dried red chilies, crushed (optional)

**1** Heat 1 tablespoon of the oil in a large wok or frying pan over medium heat and stir-fry the prawns for 1 to 2 minutes, or until the prawns turn pink. Remove and set aside.
**2** Add the remaining oil to the pan and increase the heat. Add the garlic and cook for 20 seconds, then add the noodles and stir-fry for 2 to 3 minutes. Stir in the sweet black soy sauce. Return the prawns to the pan and stir in the fish sauce, oyster sauce, basil leaves and chilies. Place on a serving platter. Serve hot.

To make this dish a success, use the fresh wide rice noodles, sold at Asian markets. These are best when freshly made, but older noodles can be freshened by plunging them into boiling water to soften.

Serves 4
Preparation time: **10 mins**
Cooking time: **10 mins**

# Classic Pad Thai Noodles (Kuay Tiaw Pad Thai)

This recipe calls for a dark and sweet tamarind-based sauce which gives the noodles their amber color. Do not take any shortcuts, omit any ingredients or double the recipe in an effort to make more in less time; it won't work. If you plan to make this for company, cook the noodles ahead and add bean sprouts and garlic chives when you reheat the noodles.

4 tablespoons oil, plus extra as needed
2 tablespoons chopped garlic
3 tablespoon dried prawns
1 tablespoon chopped preserved salted radish (page 4)
250 g (8 oz) pork loin, sliced
250 g (8 oz) fresh prawns, cleaned and shelled
500 g (1 lb) fresh rice stick noodles (*kway teow* or *hofun*) or 250 g (8 oz) dried rice stick noodles, blanched for 2 minutes in boiling water and drained
2 large eggs
1 red finger-length chili, ground
20 g (¹/₂ cup) garlic chives (*gu cai*), sliced
2 tablespoons ground roasted peanuts
250 g (8 oz) bean sprouts
¹/₂ teaspoon ground chilies, or more to taste
Freshly squeezed lime juice, to taste

Serves 2
Preparation time: 15 mins
Cooking time: 10 mins

**Pad Thai Sauce**
3 tablespoons tamarind pulp soaked in 1 cup (250 ml) water, mashed and strained to obtain the juice
185 g (1 cup) shaved palm sugar (if unavailable, use dark brown sugar and add 2 tablespoons coconut milk)
250 ml (1 cup) water
125 ml (¹/₂ cup) fish sauce

1 To make the Pad Thai Sauce, mix all the ingredients in a saucepan and simmer for about 45 minutes until well mixed and syrupy, stirring occasionally. Store any leftovers in the refrigerator in a tightly sealed container.
2 Heat the oil in a wok over medium to high heat. Add the garlic and stir-fry until golden brown. Add the dried prawns and salted turnip and stir a few times. Add the pork and prawns and keep stirring until the prawns change color. Remove the prawns to prevent over-cooking and set aside.
3 Add the noodles to the wok. They will stick together so stir quickly to separate them. Add ¹/₂ cup of the Pad Thai Sauce and keep stirring until everything is thoroughly mixed. Add more sauce as desired. The noodles should appear soft and moist. If they look hard, add a little more Sauce or cold water and stir again. Return the cooked prawns to the wok.
4 Push the contents of the wok up around the sides to make room for frying the eggs. If the pan is very dry, add 1 more tablespoon oil. Add the eggs and spread the noodles over them to cover. When the eggs are cooked, stir the noodles until everything is well mixed—there should be cooked bits of egg white and yolk throughout the noodle mixture.
5 Mix in the chilies, garlic chives and half the bean-sprouts. Remove to a platter. Sprinkle with the ground peanuts and remaining raw bean sprouts and a few drops of fresh lime juice.

# Prawns with Glass Noodles
## (Gung Ob Wun Sen)

220 g (7$^1/_2$ oz) glass noodles, soaked 20 minutes,
  drained and cut into lengths (page 50)
250 g (8 oz) fresh medium prawns, peeled and deveined
1 sprig fresh coriander leaves, coarsely chopped,
  for garnish (optional)

**First Seasonings**
4 cloves garlic, peeled and crushed
3 fresh coriander roots, crushed
2$^1/_2$ cm (1 in) fresh ginger, crushed
1 teaspoon Sichuan peppercorns (see note)

**Second Seasonings**
250 ml (1 cup) chicken stock
2 tablespoons oil
1 tablespoon oyster sauce
1 tablespoon dark soy sauce

**1** Line a claypot with the First Seasonings. Arrange the
noodles on top. Put the prawns on top of the noodles.
**2** Pour the Second Seasonings over the prawns and
noodles. Cover and cook the mixture over high heat
until the prawns turn pink, about 5 minutes. Garnish
with the coriander leaves and serve from the claypot.

**Sichuan peppercorns** are also known as Chinese pepper or flower pepper (hua jiao in Mandarin). It has a
sharp pungence that tingles and slightly numbs the
lips and tongue, an effect known in Chinese as ma la
"numb hot".

Serves 4
Preparation time: **10 mins**
Cooking time: **5 mins**

# Tangy Stir-fried Rice Noodles (Mee Kati)

500 ml (2 cups) coconut milk

60 ml ($^1/_4$ cup) yellow bean paste

3 shallots, sliced

1 tablespoon tomato paste or ketchup

200 g (1 cup) lean minced pork

375 g (12 oz) fresh prawns, peeled and coarsely chopped

50 g ($^1/_4$ cup) sugar

2 tablespoons tamarind pulp soaked in 60 ml ($^1/_4$ cup) water, mashed and strained to obtain the juice

3 tablespoons fish sauce

500 g (1 lb) dried rice vermicelli (*beehoon* or *mifen*), soaked for 5 minutes and drained

40 g (1 cup) snipped garlic chives (*gu cai*)

250 g (8 oz) bean sprouts

1 tablespoon oil

2 eggs, lightly beaten (optional)

**1** Heat the coconut milk in a wok or large saucepan over high heat. When it boils, add the yellow bean paste, shallots, tomato paste and minced pork. Stir well to combine. Reduce the heat to medium and cook until the mixture comes to a boil.

**2** Stir in the sugar, tamarind juice and fish sauce, making sure to break up any clumps of meat, then add the prawns and cook until they turn pink. Stir in the noodles, mix well and continue cooking until the sauce is absorbed. If the noodles do not soften completely, stir in some water and cook a little longer. Stir in the bean sprouts and garlic chives and mix them well. Remove to a serving platter.

**3** Heat the oil in a wok over medium–high heat. Stir in the eggs and cook through without stirring until firm. Slide the omelet from the pan and cut into shreds. Garnish the vermicelli with the egg shreds. Serve hot.

Serves 4 to 6
Preparation time: 10 mins
Cooking time: 20 mins

# Fried Bean Thread Noodles

4 tablespoons oil
3 cloves garlic, chopped
250 g (8 oz) thinly sliced pork, beef or chicken
3 tablespoons wood ear mushrooms, soaked in hot water for 20 minutes, and stems removed
1 carrot, peeled and finely shredded
1 stalk Chinese celery, shredded (see note)
200 g (7 oz) dried glass noodles, soaked 10 minutes, drained, and cut into lengths
$1/4$ cup (60 ml) chicken stock or cold water
2 large eggs, lightly beaten
1 tablespoon vinegar
3 tablespoons fish sauce
1 teaspoon sugar
$1/2$ teaspoon salt
$1/2$ teaspoon freshly ground black pepper
2 spring onions, cut into lengths

**1** Heat 3 tablespoons of the oil in a wok over medium-high heat. Stir-fry the garlic until light brown, 2 to 3 minutes. Add the meat, and stir-fry until the meat cooks through, 2 to 3 minutes.
**2** Add the mushrooms, carrots, and celery. Stir until well mixed. Stir in the noodles, then the stock and mix well. Push the noodles up onto the sides of the pan.
**3** Add the remaining oil. Pour in the eggs and scramble them, then mix with the contents of the pan. Stir in the vinegar, fish sauce, sugar, salt, pepper, and spring onions. Remove to a serving platter.

**Chinese celery** is much smaller with thinner stems than the normal Western variety and has a very intense, parsley-like flavor. The leaves and sometimes the stems are added to soups, rice dishes and stir-fried vegetables.

Serves 2
Preparation time: **10 mins**
Cooking time: **15 mins**

# Chicken Curry Noodles (Khao Soi Gai)

625 ml (2$^1/_2$ cups) coconut milk

500 g (1 lb) boneless chicken meat, cut into bite-sized pieces

2 tablespoons fish sauce

$^1/_2$ teaspoon salt

$^1/_2$ teaspoon sugar

500 ml (2 cups) oil

500 g (1 lb) dried egg noodles

1 spring onion, finely chopped

1 sprig fresh coriander leaves, coarsely chopped

1 large lime or lemon, cut in wedges

**Curry Paste**

2 teaspoons coriander seeds

2 dried red chilies

$^1/_2$ medium onion, coarsely chopped

6 cloves garlic, peeled

5 thin slices fresh ginger

3 cardamom pods, smash the pods and remove the seeds, discard the pods

$^1/_2$ teaspoon ground nutmeg

$^1/_4$ teaspoon ground mace

3 whole cloves

2 teaspoons curry powder

$^1/_2$ teaspoon dried shrimp paste (*belachan*)

60 ml ($^1/_4$ cup) water, or more as needed

**1** To make the Curry Paste, first roast the coriander and caraway seeds in a dry frying-pan over medium heat until fragrant, about 2 minutes. Next, combine with all the remaining ingredients in a blender and process until smooth, adding water as needed.

**2** In a large saucepan or wok, heat 375 ml (1$^1/_2$ cups) of the coconut milk over medium heat. When it comes to a boil, stir in the Curry Paste and cook until fragrant, about 5 minutes.

**3** Add the chicken and stir well to mix. When the curry comes to a boil again, add the remaining coconut milk, fish sauce, salt and sugar. Cover, reduce the heat to low and cook until the chicken is tender, about 20 minutes.

**4** Heat the oil in a large wok or saucepan over medium heat. Deep-fry about 105 g (4 oz) of the noodles until golden brown. Remove with a slotted spoon. Drain on paper towels and set aside.

**5** Cook the remaining noodles in boiling water until tender, about 3 minutes. Drain and arrange the noodles in individual serving bowls.

**6** To serve, pour the curry into a large tureen. Ladle the sauce over the top of each portion. Garnish each serving with the fried noodles, spring onions and coriander leaves. Squeeze a wedge of lime over the top before eating.

If preferred, beef may be used as a substitute for chicken meat. Cook for about 50 minutes.

Serves 4
Preparation time: **20 mins**
Cooking time: **25 mins**

# Crispy Noodles with Pork (Mee Krob)

3 tablespoons oil plus 500 ml (2 cups) for deep-frying
1 onion, diced
3 cloves garlic, minced
2 teaspoons yellow bean paste
2 tablespoons tomato paste or ketchup
50 g ($^1/_4$ cup) sugar
60 ml ($^1/_4$ cup) fish sauce
2 tablespoons tamarind pulp soaked in 60 ml ($^1/_4$ cup) water, mashed and strained to obtain the juice)
Juice from 1 lemon
Grated rind from 1 lemon
150 g ($^3/_4$ cup) lean pork loin, thinly sliced
500 g (1 lb) dried rice vermicelli (*beehoon* or *mifen*), soaked for 5 minutes and drained
40 g (1 cup) snipped garlic chives (*gu cai*) or 2 spring onions, cut into lengths
250 g (8 oz) fresh bean sprouts (optional)
Lemon wedges (optional)

**1** Heat 3 tablespoons of oil in a wok over medium–high heat. Stir-fry the onion, garlic, yellow bean paste, and tomato paste until fragrant, about 3 minutes.

**2** Add the sugar, fish sauce, and tamarind juice, and bring to a boil. Stir in the lemon juice, lemon rind, and pork. Reduce the heat to low and cook uncovered for about 30 minutes, stirring occasionally.

**3** Meanwhile, heat 500 ml (2 cups) of oil in a large saucepan over medium–high heat. Add the noodles, one handful at a time, to the oil in a single layer. Fry one side until golden and carefully turn the layer of noodles over to fry the other side. Remove the noodles and drain them on paper towels. Repeat until all the noodles are fried.

**4** Arrange the fried noodles on a serving platter, ladle the meat and sauce over them, and garnish with the garlic chives. Surround the noodles with the bean sprouts and garnish with the lemon wedges, if desired. Serve hot.

Serves 4 to 6
Preparation time: 10 mins
Cooking time: 40 mins

# Beef Kuay Tiaw Noodles with Chinese Broccoli

2 shallots, coarsely chopped
2 dried red chilies
125 ml ($^1/_2$ cup) coconut milk
125 ml ($^1/_2$ cup) water
500 g (1 lb) fresh rice stick noodles (*kway teow* or *hofun*)
  or 250 g (8 oz) dried rice stick noodles, blanched for
  2 minutes in boiling water and drained
250 g (8 oz) thinly sliced beef
500 g (1 lb) Chinese broccoli (see note) or Western
  broccoli, stems peeled and sliced
2 tablespoons tamarind pulp soaked in 60 ml ($^1/_4$ cup)
  water, mashed and strained to obtain the juice
2 tablespoons sugar
2 tablespoons sweet black soy sauce
4 tablespoons fish sauce

**1** Using a pestle and mortar, pound the shallots and chilies until smooth.
**2** Heat the coconut milk and water in a large wok or frying-pan over medium heat until it comes to a boil. Add the shallot mixture and cook, stirring, for 2 to 3 minutes.
**3** Add the noodles, beef, Chinese broccoli, tamarind juice, sugar, sweet black soy sauce and fish sauce, and stir to combine. Remove to a serving platter. Serve hot.

Chinese broccoli, also known as *kailan* or Chinese kale, has long, narrow stems and leaves, and small edible flowers. The stems are the tastiest part while the leaves are slightly bitter and are often discarded. Chinese broccoli is available fresh in Asian markets. Substitute with broccoli stems or broccolini.

Serves 4
Preparation time: **10 mins**
Cooking time: **10 mins**

# Rice Stick Noodles with Meat Sauce
## (Kuay Tiaw Nua Sap)

250 g (8 oz) fresh rice stick noodles (*kway teow* or *hofun*) or 125 g (4 oz) dried rice stick noodles, blanched for 2 minutes in boiling water and drained
1 tablespoon sweet black soy sauce
1 teaspoon curry powder
2 tablespoons cornstarch
2 tablespoons fish sauce
250 g (8 oz) lean minced beef
4 tablespoons oil
80 g (1 cups) leafy green lettuce, torn
3 cloves garlic, peeled and minced
375 ml (1$^1$/$_2$ cups) chicken or beef stock
2 sprigs fresh coriander leaves, coarsely chopped

**1** Drain the noodles well, place in a bowl, separate them and sprinkle with the sweet black soy sauce. Set aside.
**2** Combine the curry powder, cornstarch and fish sauce in a mixing bowl. Stir in the minced beef and set aside.
**3** Heat 3 tablespoons of the oil in a wok or frying-pan over medium heat. Stir in the noodles and cook for 3 or 4 minutes, or until heated through. Line a serving platter with the lettuce leaves and place the noodles on top.
**4** Add the remaining oil to the wok and stir-fry the garlic until brown. Add the beef and stir-fry for 2 to 3 minutes. Stir in the stock. Pour the meat mixture over the noodles and garnish with the fresh coriander leaves.

Serves 2
Preparation time: **15 mins**
Cooking time: **10 mins**

# Rice Noodles with Vegetables

3 tablespoons oil

3 cloves garlic, peeled and minced

250 g (8 oz) beef, pork or chicken, thinly sliced

250 g (8 oz) fresh rice stick noodles (*kway teow* or *hofun*) or 125 g (4 oz) dried rice stick noodles, blanched for 2 minutes in boiling water and drained

125 ml ($^1/_2$ cup) chicken stock

200 g (2 cups) shredded cabbage

250 g (8 oz) bean sprouts

120 g (1 cup) broccoli, or *bok choy*, chopped

2 spring onions, cut into lengths

60 ml ($^1/_4$ cup) Chili-Vinegar (see note)

**Sauce**

1 tablespoon yellow bean paste

1 tablespoon fish sauce

1 tablespoon sweet black soy sauce

1 tablespoon oyster sauce

1 teaspoon sugar

**1** To make the Sauce, combine the ingredients in a small bowl and set aside.

**2** Heat the oil in a wok or frying pan over medium–high heat. Stir-fry the garlic until light brown, 2 to 3 minutes. Add the meat and stir-fry until it cooks through, 2 to 3 minutes.

**3** Add the noodles and the Sauce. Stir to mix well. Add the stock and all the vegetables. Stir-fry until the noodles are moist and soft, about 3 minutes.

**4** Spoon the mixture onto a serving platter. Serve with the Chili-Vinegar, if desired.

To make the **Chili-Vinegar**, slice several green chilies into circles, put them in a small bowl and cover with cider vinegar.

Serves 4
Preparation time: **10 mins**
Cooking time: **10 mins**

# Kuay Tiaw Noodles with Broccoli

500 g (1 lb) Chinese broccoli or regular broccoli (see note)

5 tablespoons oil

500 g (1 lb) fresh rice stick noodles (*kway teow* or *hofun*) or 250 g (8 oz) dried rice stick noodles, blanched for 2 minutes in boiling water and drained

1 tablespoon dark soy sauce

1 large egg, beaten

3 cloves garlic, chopped

250 g (8 oz) chicken or pork, thinly sliced, or fresh prawns, shelled and deveined

1 tablespoon yellow bean paste

1 to 2 tablespoons fish sauce

375 ml (1 $^1$/$_2$ cups) chicken stock

1 tablespoon cornstarch mixed with 2 tablespoons water

$^1$/$_4$ teaspoon ground white pepper

**a1** Cut the broccoli into lengths. Peel the tough stems and cut to the same size as the leafy portions.

**2** Heat 2 tablespoons of the oil in a wok over high heat. Add the noodles and soy sauce and stir-fry for about 30 seconds. Push the noodles to the sides of the pan and add the egg. Stir the egg and noodles together and transfer to a serving platter.

**3** Add the remaining oil to the same pan and heat. Add the garlic and stir-fry until golden, then stir-fry the meat until it changes color. Stir in the bean sauce and the fish sauce.

**4** Stir in the greens, chicken stock, and cornstarch mixture, and continue cooking and stirring until the sauce is transparent. Pour the mixture over the noodles and sprinkle with the ground white pepper.

**Chinese broccoli**, also known as *kailan* or Chinese kale, has long, narrow stems and leaves, and small edible flowers. The stems are the tastiest part while the leaves are slightly bitter and are often discarded. Chinese broccoli is available fresh in Asian markets. Substitute with broccoli stems or broccolini.

Serves 4
Preparation time: **15 mins**
Cooking time: **10 mins**

# Index

**Dips, Sauces and Condiments**
*Ajaad* 6
Cucumber Salad 6
*Miang Kham Sauce* 7
*Nam Jim* 6
*Nam Prik Kang Phet* 7
Red Curry Paste 7
Sweet and Hot Plum Sauce 6

**Noodle Soups**
Beef Kuay Tiaw Noodles with
  Chinese Broccoli 57
Chicken Curry Noodles 53
Chicken Noodle Soup 34
Classic Pad Thai Noodles 44
Crispy Noodles with Pork 54
Duck Noodle Soup 36
Fried Bean Thread Noodles 50
Fried Rice Noodles with Prawns and
  Thai Basil 42
*Gung Ob Wun Sen* 47
*Khao Soi Gai* 53
*Kuay Tiaw Gai* 34
*Kuay Tiaw Nua Puai* 38
*Kuay Tiaw Nua Sap* 58
*Kuay Tiaw Pad Thai* 44
*Kuay Tiaw Ped* 36
Tangy Stir-fried Rice Noodles 48
Tender Fragrant Beef Noodle Soup 38
*Mee Kati* 48
*Mee Krob* 54
Kuay Tiaw Noodles with Broccoli 63
Rice Stick Noodles with Meat Sauce 58
Prawn and Pineapple Noodle Salad 40
Prawns with Glass Noodles 47
Rice Noodles with Vegetables 60

**Snacks**
Chicken Curry Puffs 20
Crispy Rice Crackers with Dip 18
Fresh Spring Rolls 8
Fried Beancurd with Sweet and Hot
  Sauce 33
Fried Corn Patties 25
Fried Spring Rolls 30
Golden Cups 22
Golden Sacks 26
*Kari Puff* 20
*Khanom Jeeb*, 12
*Khao Tang Na Tang* 18
*Kratong Thong* 22
*Kung Hom Pha* 15
Lettuce Leaf Cups 10
*Miang Kham* 10
*Po Piah Sot* 8
*Po Piah Todd* 30
Prawns in a Blanket 15
*Puu Jaa* 14
*Saté Muu* 16
Steamed Prawn Dumplings 12
Steamed Mussels with Lemongrass 24
Thai Crab Cakes 14
Thai Fish Cakes 27
Thai Pork Satay 16
*Taohu Saweai* 33
Tapioca Dumplings with Pork
  Filling 27
*Tod Man Khao Pote* 25
*Tod Man Pla* 27
*Tung Thong* 26